The Pampered Chef®
discover the chef in you...

# Grill it Quick!

Don't wait until the weekend to prepare a great meal on the grill! In this recipe collection, you'll find quick and simple main dish recipes that are perfect for any night of the week. Simply preheat your grill, and dinner will be ready in 30 minutes from start to finish. We've also designed side dishes to keep your kitchen cool that are cooked on the grill, in the microwave, or not cooked at all. So, fire up the grill, and Grill it Quick!

Enjoy!
The Pampered Chef® Test Kitchens

On the front cover: Jamaican Sea Bass with Mango & Black Bean Salad, p. 19.

"About Our Recipes" and "Notes on Nutrition" can be found on our Web site at www.pamperedchef.com under Products, Etc.

**LIGHT** • Look for this symbol to find our recipes that contain 30 percent or fewer calories from fat.

# contents

# Peel & Eat Barbecue Prawns

Keeping the shells on shrimp helps to keep them moist and heightens their flavor during grilling.

### Shrimp

- 2 tbsp (30 mL) **Smoky Barbecue Rub**
- 2 tbsp (30 mL) olive oil
- 1 tbsp (15 mL) Louisiana hot sauce
- 2 garlic cloves, pressed
- 16 jumbo uncooked shell-on shrimp (13-15 per pound), deveined (see Chef's Corner)
- 8 12-in. (30-cm) bamboo skewers, soaked (see Chef's Corner)

### Corn Relish

- 4 ears fresh corn, husks and silk removed, or 3 cups (750 mL) frozen corn kernels, thawed
- ½ medium red bell pepper
- 2 green onions with tops (about ½ cup/125 mL sliced)
- 3 tbsp (45 mL) prepared coleslaw dressing

**Prep time:** 20 minutes  **Total time:** 30 minutes

1. Prepare grill for direct cooking over medium-high heat. For shrimp, combine rub, oil, hot sauce and garlic pressed with **Garlic Press** in **Stainless (4-qt./4-L) Mixing Bowl**. Add shrimp; toss to coat and refrigerate until ready to grill.

2. For relish, cut off ends of ears of corn, creating a flat base. Stand upright on cutting board and remove kernels with **Santoku Knife**. Dice bell pepper and slice green onions. Combine corn, bell pepper, green onions and coleslaw dressing in **Classic Batter Bowl**. Cover and refrigerate.

3. Lay shrimp flat on **Cutting Board**; thread four pieces of shrimp evenly down length of one skewer. Holding shrimp steady, insert a second skewer parallel to the first skewer. Repeat with remaining shrimp and six additional skewers.

4. Grill shrimp 3 minutes or until shells are blackened on one side. Turn using **BBQ Tongs**; grill 3-5 minutes or until shells are blackened and shrimp are opaque throughout. Serve shrimp with relish.

**Yield:** 4 servings

U.S. Nutrients per serving: Calories 290, Total Fat 13 g, Saturated Fat 1.5 g, Cholesterol 85 mg, Carbohydrate 22 g, Protein 26 g, Sodium 990 mg, Fiber 3 g
U.S. Diabetic exchanges per serving: 1 starch, 1 vegetable, 3 low-fat meat, ½ fat (1 carb)

## chef's corner

Double skewers keep the shrimp from spinning when you turn the kebabs on the grill. Soak skewers in water for at least 2 hours to prevent burning.

Most shrimp can be purchased deveined with shells still intact. You can also do this yourself. Using a small serrated knife, cut along the back of the shrimp and lift out the vein.

You can find bottled coleslaw dressing in the salad dressing aisle of your grocery store. You can make a homemade version by combining 3 tbsp (45 mL) mayonnaise, 1 tsp (5 mL) cider vinegar, 1 tsp (5 mL) sugar and ⅛ tsp (0.5 mL) salt.

# Mojito Chicken Salad

In the time it takes to reduce the syrup for the flavorful mojito-inspired salad dressing, the rest of the salad ingredients can be prepared and the chicken ready to grill.

### Dressing

- 1 can (15 oz/398 mL) mandarin oranges in light syrup, undrained
- 3 tbsp (45 mL) sugar
- 2 limes
- 3 tbsp (45 mL) chopped fresh mint leaves
- ¼ tsp (1 mL) ground cayenne pepper
- 3 tbsp (45 mL) olive oil

### Chicken and Salad

- 4 boneless, skinless chicken breasts (4-6 oz/125-175 g each)
- ½ tsp (2 mL) salt
- ¼ tsp (1 mL) coarsely ground black pepper
- 4 cups (1 L) baby spring mix salad blend

**Prep time:** 20 minutes   **Total time:** 30 minutes

1. Prepare grill for direct cooking over medium-high heat. For dressing, drain syrup from mandarin oranges into **Small Batter Bowl**; stir in sugar (set aside oranges for salad). Microwave on HIGH 10-12 minutes or until syrup is thickened and reduced by half (about 6 tbsp/90 mL). Zest limes to measure 2 tsp (10 mL) zest; juice limes into batter bowl. Add lime zest, chopped mint, cayenne pepper and oil. Reserve ¼ cup (50 mL) of the dressing in **Prep Bowl** for brushing over chicken. Refrigerate remaining dressing for salad.

2. For chicken, season chicken with salt and black pepper. Grill chicken, covered, 5 minutes or until grill marks appear. Turn chicken over; brush with reserved dressing and grill 5-7 minutes or until **Pocket Thermometer** registers 170°F (77°C) in thickest part of breast and juices run clear. (Discard any remaining dressing used for brushing on chicken.) Transfer chicken from grill to **Large Grooved Cutting Board**; let stand 5 minutes.

3. For salad, toss salad blend with 2 tbsp (30 mL) of the dressing; divide evenly among serving plates. Cut chicken into thin slices; arrange over salad. Top with reserved mandarin oranges. Drizzle with remaining dressing.

**Yield:** 4 servings

U.S. Nutrients per serving: Calories 300, Total Fat 12 g, Saturated Fat 2 g, Cholesterol 65 mg, Carbohydrate 23 g, Protein 28 g, Sodium 380 mg, Fiber 2 g
U.S. Diabetic exchanges per serving: 1½ fruit, 4 low-fat meat (1½ carb)

## chef's corner

The syrup from the mandarin oranges is used in the dressing to sweeten and thicken it slightly. Microwave the syrup and sugar mixture until it is reduced by half. Juice the limes directly into the batter bowl using the **Citrus Press**.

Mandarin oranges come in different sizes of cans and jars. For this recipe, the syrup should measure about ¾ cup (175 mL) and the oranges should measure about 1 cup (250 mL).

# Portobello, Red Pepper & Goat Cheese Pizza

The crust of this robust, meatless pizza is grilled on both sides, doubling the great grilled flavor.

**Vinaigrette**

- ¼ cup (50 mL) **Garlic Oil** or olive oil
- 2 tbsp (30 mL) red wine vinegar
- 2 garlic cloves, pressed
- 1 tsp (5 mL) finely chopped fresh thyme leaves
- ½ tsp (2 mL) salt
- ¼ tsp (1 mL) coarsely ground black pepper

**Pizza**

- 12 oz (350 g) portobello mushrooms (about 6 medium)
- 1 medium red bell pepper
- 1 10-oz (300-g) prebaked thin pizza crust
- 1 pkg (4 oz/125 g) crumbled goat cheese, divided

**Prep time:** 20 minutes   **Total time:** 30 minutes

1. Prepare grill for direct cooking over medium-high heat. For vinaigrette, whisk together ingredients in **Small Batter Bowl**. Reserve 2 tbsp (30 mL) in **Prep Bowl** for serving.

2. For pizza, remove stems from mushrooms with **Paring Knife** and cut bell pepper in half. Brush both sides of pizza crust with vinaigrette. Grill vegetables, covered, 8-9 minutes or until tender, turning and brushing occasionally with vinaigrette using **BBQ Basting Brush**. Remove vegetables from grill.

3. Place pizza crust top side down onto grid of grill. Grill, covered, 1-2 minutes or until slighly browned and crisp. Turn crust over with **BBQ Turner**; top with goat cheese, reserving 1 tbsp (15 mL) for garnish. Grill an additional 1-2 minutes or until bottom of crust is browned and crisp. (Cheese will soften but not appear melted.) Remove crust from grill.

4. Slice bell pepper into thin strips and mushrooms on a bias using **Santoku Knife**. Arrange mushrooms and bell pepper over crust. Drizzle reserved vinaigrette evenly over top. Sprinkle with reserved goat cheese, if desired.

**Yield:** 4 servings

U.S. Nutrients per serving: Calories 450, Total Fat 27 g, Saturated Fat 8 g, Cholesterol 30 mg, Carbohydrate 38 g, Protein 17 g, Sodium 810 mg, Fiber 3 g
U.S. Diabetic exchanges per serving: 2 starch, 1 vegetable, 1 high-fat meat, 4 fat (2 carb)

## chef's corner

Watch the pizza crust closely. If the crust starts to brown unevenly, rotate it on the grill as necessary.

Look for prepared thin pizza crusts in the bread aisle of your grocery store.

Crumbled feta cheese can be substituted for the crumbled goat cheese, if desired.

If desired, ¼ tsp (1 mL) dried thyme leaves can be substituted for the fresh thyme leaves in the dressing.

# Japanese-Style Salmon & Cucumber Salad

A flavorful seasoning paste is spread on the inside and outside of spiral-rolled salmon fillets.

**Seasoning Paste**

- 1 lemon, divided
- 1 1-in. (2.5-cm) piece peeled fresh gingerroot
- 2 tbsp (30 mL) **Asian Seasoning Mix**
- 1 tbsp (15 mL) soy sauce
- 1 tbsp (15 mL) toasted sesame oil
- 1 garlic clove, pressed

**Salad and Salmon Rolls**

- 2 seedless cucumbers
- ¼ cup (50 mL) seasoned rice vinegar
- 1 6-inch-wide (15-cm) center-cut salmon fillet (about 1½ lb/750 g)
- Lemon slices (optional)

**Prep time:** 20 minutes  **Toal time:** 30 minutes

1. Prepare grill for direct cooking over medium-high heat. For paste, zest lemon and grate gingerroot with **Microplane® Adjustable Grater** to measure 1 tsp (5 mL) each. Juice lemon using **Juicer** to measure 2 tbsp (30 mL) juice. In **(2-cup/500-mL) Easy Read Measuring Cup**, combine zest, 1 tbsp (15 mL) of the juice, gingerroot, seasoning mix, soy sauce, oil and garlic pressed with **Garlic Press**.

2. For salad, cut cucumbers in half crosswise using **Utility Knife**; cut into julienne strips with **Julienne Peeler** and place into **Stainless (2-qt./2-L) Mixing Bowl**. Combine remaining 1 tbsp (15 mL) lemon juice and vinegar in **Prep Bowl** and set aside for serving.

3. For rolls, cut salmon into 1½-in. (4-cm) strips using **Boning Knife**. Spread a small amount of the paste over each salmon strip, coating completely. Roll up strips and tie with butcher's twine; spread rolls with remaining paste. Grill rolls, covered, 4 minutes or until grill marks appear. Turn using **BBQ Turner**; grill 4-6 minutes or until grill marks appear and **Pocket Thermometer** registers 140°F (60°C). Remove from grill and carefully remove twine.

4. To serve, toss salad with vinegar mixture. Divide salad among serving plates; top with salmon rolls.

**Yield:** 4 servings

U.S. Nutrients per serving: Calories 370, Total Fat 22 g, Saturated Fat 4 g, Cholesterol 100 mg, Carbohydrate 6 g, Protein 35 g, Sodium 660 mg, Fiber less than 1 g
U.S. Diabetic exchanges per serving: 5 meat (0 carb)

## chef's corner

Choose a center-cut salmon fillet with an even thickness and width for this recipe. It should measure 6 in. (15 cm) wide so you can cut four narrow, 1½-in. (4-cm) strips that will be easy to roll up.

Seasoned rice vinegar is rice vinegar with sugar and salt added. It contributes a mildly sweet, tangy flavor when used in salad dressings such as this one.

To substitute Asian Seasoning Mix, increase gingerroot to 2 tsp (10 mL) and increase garlic to 2 cloves in the seasoning paste.

# Grilled Caesar Salad

This hearty main dish spin on Caesar salad includes cannellini beans. Grilled romaine lettuce hearts make for a stunning presentation.

## Vinaigrette

- ⅓ cup (75 mL) olive oil
- ¼ cup (50 mL) fresh lemon juice
- 1 tbsp (15 mL) Dijon mustard
- 2 garlic cloves, pressed
- ½ tsp (2 mL) salt
- ¼ tsp (1 mL) coarsely ground black pepper

## Salad

- 1 can (15.5 oz or 540 mL) cannellini beans, rinsed and drained
- 1 cup (250 mL) grape tomatoes, halved
- 2 tbsp (30 mL) chopped fresh parsley
- 2 romaine lettuce hearts
- 1 large red onion
- 4 slices (½ in./1 cm thick) French bread
- 1 oz (30 g) Parmesan cheese

**Prep time:** 20 minutes  **Total time:** 25 minutes

1. Prepare grill for direct cooking over medium-high heat. For vinaigrette, whisk together ingredients in **Small Batter Bowl**. For salad, combine beans, tomatoes, parsley and 3 tbsp (45 mL) of the vinaigrette in **Classic Batter Bowl**; toss to coat and set aside.

2. Cut romaine hearts in half horizontally with **Santoku Knife**, keeping cores intact. Wash lettuce (see Chef's Corner). Cut onion crosswise into 1-inch-thick (2.5-cm) slices. Brush lettuce and onion slices with remaining vinaigrette using **Chef's Silicone Basting Brush**.

3. Grill onion slices 3 minutes or until grill marks appear. Turn using **BBQ Turner**. Add lettuce and bread slices; grill 2-3 minutes or until grill marks appear and edges are slightly charred, turning occasionally. Remove from grill.

4. Slice bread into ½-in. (1-cm) cubes. Place romaine halves onto serving plates. Top with bean mixture, onion rings and bread cubes. Grate Parmesan cheese over each serving using **Deluxe Cheese Grater**.

**Yield:** 4 servings

U.S. Nutrients per serving: Calories 460, Total Fat 22 g, Saturated Fat 4 g, Cholesterol 5 mg, Carbohydrate 52 g, Protein 13 g, Sodium 1030 mg, Fiber 7 g
U.S. Diabetic exchanges per serving: 3½ starch, ½ high-fat meat, 3 fat (3½ carb)

## chef's corner

Look for firm, tightly packed romaine hearts, which hold up best for grilling. Grill the lettuce just until grill marks appear in order to impart a smoky flavor while keeping it crisp.

To wash lettuce, cut romaine hearts in half and rinse under cold running water without separating the leaves. Gently shake out excess water and place lettuce, cut side down, onto clean kitchen towels until mostly dry. Excess water will steam the lettuce.

Cannellini beans are white kidney beans. If desired, Great Northern beans can be substituted for the cannellini beans.

# Tuscan Turkey Burgers

Adding Italian dressing and Italian sausage to the ground turkey adds great flavor to these mouthwatering burgers.

½ cup (125 mL) fresh bread
    crumbs

¼ cup (50 mL) Italian salad
    dressing

2 garlic cloves, pressed

1 lb (500 g) 93% lean ground
    turkey

8 oz (250 g) hot Italian turkey
    sausage, casings removed

¼ cup (50 mL) finely chopped
    fresh basil, divided

1 focaccia bread round
    (about 12 oz/350 g)

*Pesto Mayonnaise* (optional,
    see Chef's Corner)

1 medium plum tomato, sliced

**Prep time:** 15 minutes   **Total time:** 30 minutes

1. Prepare grill for direct cooking over medium-high heat. Combine bread crumbs, dressing and garlic pressed with **Garlic Press** in **Stainless (4-qt./4-L) Mixing Bowl**. Add turkey, sausage and half of the basil. Mix gently but thoroughly with **Mix 'N Scraper®**.

2. Form mixture into four round patties, about 1 in. (2.5 cm) thick. Grill, covered, 5 minutes or until grill marks appear. Turn burgers over using **BBQ Turner**; grill 5-7 minutes or until centers of burgers are no longer pink and **Pocket Thermometer** registers 165°F (74°C). Remove burgers from grill.

3. Meanwhile, cut focaccia bread in half horizontally with **Bread Knife**. Place, cut side down, onto grid of grill. Grill 1 minute or until lightly toasted. Remove from grill and cut into quarters. Spread with *Pesto Mayonnaise*, if desired. Serve burgers in focaccia. Top with remaining basil and tomato slices.

**Yield:** 4 burgers

U.S. Nutrients per serving: Calories 540, Total Fat 21 g, Saturated Fat 4.5 g, Cholesterol 100 mg, Carbohydrate 52 g, Protein 38 g, Sodium 1210 mg, Fiber 2 g
U.S. Diabetic exchanges per serving: 3½ starch, 4 medium-fat meat, 1 fat (3½ carb)

## chef's corner

Prevent tough burgers by mixing the ingredients just until they are combined. Break up the sausage over the turkey so that it combines quickly without over-mixing.

For *Pesto Mayonnaise*, combine 2 tbsp (30 mL) mayonnaise and 1 tbsp (15 mL) prepared basil pesto.

Soaking the bread crumbs in salad dressing tenderizes the burgers.

Placing your formed burger patties onto squares of foil makes it easy to transfer them to the grill. Carefully invert the patty onto the grid of the grill and peel off foil.

# Tandoori-Style Lamb Chops

These lamb chops are seasoned with richly flavored red curry powder and served with a quick version of a traditional Indian bread called naan.

### Yogurt Marinade and Sauce

- 1 cup (250 mL) plain yogurt
- 1 tbsp (15 mL) red curry powder
- 1 tbsp (15 mL) lemon juice
- 1 tbsp (15 mL) honey
- 1 tbsp (15 mL) chopped fresh parsley
- 2 garlic cloves, pressed
- 1/2 tsp (2 mL) salt

### Lamb Chops

- 8 bone-in lamb loin chops, cut 1-1½ in. (2.5-3 cm) thick (3½-4 oz/99-125 g each)

- *Grilled Bread* (optional, see Chef's Corner)

**Prep time:** 15 minutes    **Total time:** 30 minutes

1. Prepare grill for direct cooking over medium-high heat. For marinade and sauce, whisk together ingredients in **Small Batter Bowl**. Place ½ cup (125 mL) of the marinade into **Prep Bowl**; cover and refrigerate until ready to serve as sauce.

2. For lamb, trim excess fat from lamb chops. Place chops into remaining marinade; turn to coat. Cover; refrigerate until ready to grill.

3. Grill chops, covered, 4 minutes or until grill marks appear. Turn with **BBQ Tongs** and grill 4-6 minutes or until **Pocket Thermometer** registers 155°F (68°C) for medium doneness. Transfer chops from grill to serving platter; tent with foil and let stand 10 minutes (temperature will rise about 5°F).

4. Serve lamb chops with reserved yogurt sauce and *Grilled Bread*, if desired.

**Yield:** 4 servings

U.S. Nutrients per serving: Calories 430, Total Fat 28 g, Saturated Fat 12 g, Cholesterol 120 mg, Carbohydrate 11 g, Protein 33 g, Sodium 420 mg, Fiber less than 1 g
U.S. Diabetic exchanges per serving: ½ milk, ½ fruit, 4 medium-fat meat, 2 fat (1 carb)

## chef's corner

For *Grilled Bread*, combine 2 tbsp (30 mL) melted butter, 1 pressed garlic clove and ¼ tsp (1 mL) salt in Prep Bowl. Add 2 tbsp (30 mL) chopped fresh parsley. Unroll 1 pkg (13.8 oz/283 g) refrigerated pizza crust onto foil and slice crosswise into four equal strips using **Pizza Cutter**. Carefully invert the crust onto the grid of the grill and peel off foil. Grill bread 2-4 minutes, brushing with butter mixture and turning often to avoid burning.

Red curry powder is a blend of ground red chili peppers and spices. Yellow curry powder can be substituted for the red curry powder, if desired.

# Teriyaki Ribs with Grilled Pineapple

Great ribs don't need hours of preparation. With the help of the microwave oven, these sweet and tangy ribs are ready in only 30 minutes from start to finish.

### Pineapple and Ribs

- 1 pineapple
- 1 rack (2½-3 lb/1.1-1.4 kg) pork loin back ribs (baby back ribs)
- 1 tsp (5 mL) salt
- ¼ tsp (1 mL) coarsely ground black pepper
- ¼ cup (50 mL) water

### Sauce

- ½ cup (125 mL) teriyaki baste and glaze
- ½ cup (125 mL) pineapple preserves
- ¼ cup (50 mL) ketchup
- 1 garlic clove, pressed
- ¼-½ tsp (1-2 mL) cayenne pepper

**Prep time:** 25 minutes    **Total time:** 30 minutes

1. Prepare grill for direct cooking over medium-high heat. For pineapple, cut off top and bottom of pineapple, creating a flat base; slice off rind from top to bottom. Cut pineapple crosswise into ½-in. (1-cm) slices; remove core using **The Corer**™. Cut slices in half.

2. For ribs, remove membrane from rack of ribs using **Boning Knife** (see Chef's Corner). Season both sides of ribs with salt and black pepper. Cut between each bone to separate rack into individual ribs. Arrange ribs, cut side down, in two layers in **Deep Covered Baker**. Add water. Microwave, covered, on HIGH 8 minutes. Turn ribs over. Microwave on HIGH 7-10 minutes or until **Pocket Thermometer** registers 160°F (71°C) when inserted into meatiest part of ribs alongside bones and ribs are no longer pink.

3. Meanwhile, for sauce, combine ingredients in **Small Batter Bowl**. Reserve ½ cup (125 mL) of the sauce. Pour remaining sauce into **Stainless (4-qt./4-L) Mixing Bowl**; add cooked ribs and toss to coat.

4. Grill ribs and pineapple slices 5-7 minutes or until grill marks appear, turning and brushing occasionally with reserved sauce.

**Yield:** 4 servings

U.S. Nutrients per serving: Calories 750, Total Fat 40 g, Saturated Fat 15 g, Cholesterol 160 mg, Carbohydrate 56 g, Protein 40 g, Sodium 1390 mg, Fiber 2 g
U.S. Diabetic exchanges per serving: 3½ fruit, 5½ high-fat meat (3½ carb)

## chef's corner

The membrane found underneath the rack is tough and holds in excess fat. To remove the membrane, lay the rack meaty side down. Using the tip of the Boning Knife, gently cut under the membrane on one corner. Grasp the corner of the membrane and gently pull it away from the bones.

Teriyaki baste and glaze is a thickened teriyaki sauce found in the Asian section of most grocery stores. To substitute, combine ½ cup (125 mL) thin teriyaki sauce, ¼ cup (50 mL) cold water and 1 tbsp (15 mL) cornstarch in **(1.5-qt./1.5 L) Saucepan**. Bring to a boil, whisking constantly until thickened using **Silicone Sauce Whisk**.

# Jamaican Sea Bass with Mango & Black Bean Salad

Sea bass is a firm fish that fares well on the grill. Grilled mango and bell pepper add a subtle smokiness to the colorful black bean salad.

## Marinade and Sea Bass

- ¼ cup (50 mL) fresh lime juice
- 3 tbsp (45 mL) **Jamaican Jerk Rub**
- 2 tbsp (30 mL) **Garlic Oil** or olive oil
- 2 garlic cloves, pressed
- 4 boneless, skinless sea bass or halibut fillets (4-6 oz/125-175 g each)

## Black Bean Salad

- 1 large red bell pepper
- 1 large mango
- 2 medium green onions with tops (about ½ cup/175 mL thinly sliced)
- 1 can (15 oz/425 g) black beans, drained and rinsed
- Lime wedges

**Prep time:** 15 minutes    **Total time:** 25 minutes

1. Prepare grill for direct cooking over medium-high heat. For marinade, whisk together lime juice, rub, oil and garlic pressed with **Garlic Press** in **Stainless (2-qt./2-L) Mixing Bowl**. Place sea bass into resealable plastic bag; add half of the marinade. Seal bag; turn to coat and refrigerate no longer than 30 minutes.

2. Meanwhile, for salad, cut off sides from bell pepper to create four large, flat pieces, avoiding seeds. Peel mango with **Serrated Peeler**; cut flesh from both sides of flat pit, forming two halves. Thinly slice green onions. Add beans and ¼ cup (50 mL) of the onions to remaining marinade in mixing bowl; set aside.

3. Grill sea bass, bell pepper and mango, covered, 3 minutes or until grill marks appear; turn with **BBQ Turner**. Grill 4-5 minutes or until mango and bell pepper are charred and crisp-tender and **Pocket Thermometer** inserted into side of fillets registers 140°F (60°C).

4. To serve, divide salad among serving plates; top with sea bass fillets. Garnish with reserved green onions and lime wedges.

**Yield:** 4 servings

**LIGHT** • U.S. Nutrients per serving: Calories 270 (29% from fat), Total Fat 9 g, Saturated Fat 1 g, Cholesterol 50 mg, Carbohydrate 21 g, Protein 26 g, Sodium 610 mg, Fiber 5 g
U.S. Diabetic exchanges per serving: 1 starch, ½ fruit, 3 low-fat meat (1½ carb)

## chef's corner

When grilling mangoes, choose fruit that is slightly underripe. The heat from the grill softens the fruit and intensifies the sweetness.

To prepare the mango, determine the direction of the pit by rubbing the top part of the mango with your thumb. Slice flesh from both sides of the flat pit, forming two halves. If desired, trim additional mango flesh from the pit and add it to the salad.

Because sea bass breaks up into large flakes, don't test for doneness by flaking it with a fork. Instead, insert the Pocket Thermometer into the side of the fillet.

# Balsamic-Glazed Strip Steaks

Start grilling the steaks when the mushrooms are halfway done to get this quick bistro-style dish on the table without delay.

**Balsamic Glaze**

- 2/3 cup (150 mL) balsamic vinegar
- 1 tbsp (15 mL) olive oil
- 1 garlic clove, pressed

**Mushroom Mixture**

- 1 lb (500 g) mushrooms, halved
- 2 medium onions, sliced 1/4 in. (6 mm) thick
- 1 tbsp (15 mL) olive oil
- 1 tsp (5 mL) smoked or regular paprika
- 1 tsp (5 mL) salt

**Steaks and Garnish**

- 2 beef strip steaks, cut 1 in. (2.5 cm) thick (about 10-12 oz/300-350 g each)
- 1/2 tsp (2 mL) salt
- 1/2 tsp (2 mL) coarsely ground black pepper
- 2 beefsteak tomatoes, thickly sliced
- 1/4 cup (50 mL) crumbled blue cheese

## chef's corner

Reducing the balsamic vinegar results in a sweet and tangy syrup. The syrup will boil almost to the top of the batter bowl as it reduces in the microwave. Allow the bubbles to settle for accurate measuring.

Make sure to preheat the grill basket before adding mushrooms and onions to prevent sticking.

**Prep time:** 15 minutes     **Total time:** 30 minutes

1. Prepare grill for direct cooking over medium-high heat. For glaze, whisk together ingredients in **Small Batter Bowl**. Microwave, uncovered, on HIGH 6-8 minutes or until mixture is thick, syrupy and reduced to about 1/4 cup/50 mL.

2. For mushroom mixture, in **Stainless (4-qt./4-L) Mixing Bowl**, combine mushrooms, onions, oil, paprika and salt; mix well using **Small Mix 'N Scraper®**. Preheat **BBQ Grill Basket** on grill 3 minutes. Grill mushroom mixture, undisturbed, 7 minutes. Shake basket using **BBQ Tongs**. Grill an additional 8-9 minutes or until mushrooms are browned and onions begin to caramelize. Remove basket from grill; keep warm.

3. Set aside 2 tbsp (30 mL) glaze in **Prep Bowl** for serving. Season steaks with salt and black pepper; brush remaining glaze over both sides of steaks using **Chef's Silicone Basting Brush**. Grill steaks, covered, 4 minutes or until grill marks appear. Turn with BBQ Tongs and grill 4-6 minutes or until **Pocket Thermometer** registers 140°F (60°C) for medium-rare or 150°F (65°C) for medium doneness. Transfer steaks from grill to cutting board; tent with foil and let stand 10 minutes (temperature will rise about 5°F).

4. Slice steaks against the grain and serve with tomatoes, mushroom mixture and blue cheese. Drizzle reserved glaze over steaks.

**Yield:** 4 servings

U.S. Nutrients per serving: Calories 410, Total Fat 19 g, Saturated Fat 6 g, Cholesterol 90 mg, Carbohydrate 23 g, Protein 37 g, Sodium 1100 mg, Fiber 4 g
U.S. Diabetic exchanges per serving: 1½ fruit, 5 low-fat meat, 1 fat (1½ carb)

# Adobo-Glazed Barbecue Chicken

Adobo sauce is a thick, spicy sauce that is often used to pack chipotle peppers and adds kick to this recipe's sweet and smoky glaze.

**Chicken**

- 2 tbsp (30 mL) **Smoky Barbecue Rub**
- 2 tsp (10 mL) vegetable oil
- 2 garlic cloves, pressed
- 8 boneless, skinless chicken thighs (about 3 oz/90 g each)

**Adobo Glaze and Garnish**

- 1-2 tbsp (15-30 mL) seeded and finely chopped canned chipotle peppers (about 3-4 peppers)
- 1 tbsp (15 mL) adobo sauce from chipotle peppers
- ½ cup (125 mL) honey
- 1 tbsp (15 mL) Smoky Barbecue Rub
- 1 tbsp (15 mL) cider vinegar
- 1 medium green onion with top (about ¼ cup/50 mL sliced)

**Prep time:** 15 minutes    **Total time:** 25 minutes

1. Prepare grill for direct cooking over medium-high heat. For chicken, combine rub, oil and garlic pressed with **Garlic Press** in **Stainless (4-qt./4-L) Mixing Bowl**. Add chicken and toss to coat; cover and refrigerate until ready to grill.

2. For glaze, remove and discard seeds from chipotle peppers with **Quikut Paring Knife**; finely chop peppers with **Food Chopper**. Whisk chipotle peppers, adobo sauce, honey, rub and vinegar in **Small Batter Bowl**. Reserve half of the glaze for serving.

3. Grill chicken, covered, 4 minutes or until grill marks appear. Turn with **BBQ Tongs** and grill 4-6 minutes or until **Pocket Thermometer** inserted into thickest part of thighs registers 180°F (82°C) and juices run clear. Brush both sides of chicken with glaze using **BBQ Basting Brush** during last 2 minutes of cooking.

4. To serve, spoon reserved glaze over chicken; top with sliced green onion.

**Yield:** 4 servings

U.S. Nutrients per serving: Calories 400, Total Fat 15 g, Saturated Fat 3.5 g, Cholesterol 110 mg, Carbohydrate 37 g, Protein 31 g, Sodium 520 mg, Fiber 0 g
U.S. Diabetic exchanges per serving: 2 fruit, ½ starch, 4 low-fat meat, ½ fat (2½ carb)

## chef's corner

Make charred, glazed corn to accompany this recipe. Remove husks and silk from 4 ears of corn; discard outer husks and silk, reserving light colored inner husks. Trim ears of corn. Line bottom of **Deep Covered Baker** with half of the reserved husks. Add corn; top with remaining husks and ¼ cup (50 mL) water. Cover and microwave on HIGH 8-10 minutes or until corn is cooked through. Remove corn from baker; grill corn 4-5 minutes or until grill marks appear, brushing with some of the reserved adobo glaze.

# Citrus-Butter Shrimp Toss

While the rice pilaf cooks in the microwave, prepare and grill the shrimp and asparagus. Everything will finish cooking around the same time.

### Asparagus Pilaf

- ¼ medium yellow onion
- 1 tbsp (15 mL) butter
- 1 cup (250 mL) uncooked jasmine rice
- 1¾ cups (425 mL) chicken broth
- ½ cup (125 mL) water
- ½ tsp (2 mL) salt
- 8 oz (250 g) fresh asparagus spears, trimmed

### Shrimp

- 1 lb (500 g) medium uncooked shrimp (41-50 per pound), peeled and deveined, tails removed
- 1 tbsp (15 mL) plus 1 tsp (5 mL) **Citrus & Basil Rub**, divided
- 2 tbsp (30 mL) butter
- 1 garlic clove, pressed
- 3 tbsp (45 mL) chopped jarred pimento peppers

**Prep time:** 15 minutes    **Total time:** 30 minutes

1. Prepare grill for direct cooking over medium-high heat. For pilaf, chop onion with **Food Chopper**; place onion and butter into **Rice Cooker Plus**. Microwave onion mixture, uncovered, on HIGH 2 minutes, stirring every 30 seconds. Add rice, broth, water and salt to cooker. Microwave according to package directions.

2. For shrimp, in **Stainless (2-qt./2-L) Mixing Bowl**, toss shrimp with 1 tbsp (15 mL) of the rub. In **Classic Batter Bowl**, combine butter, remaining 1 tsp (5 mL) rub and garlic. Microwave butter mixture on HIGH 1 minute or until butter is melted; add pimentos and mix well.

3. Brush **BBQ Grill Basket** with vegetable oil; preheat on grill 3 minutes. Add shrimp and grill, covered, 4-6 minutes or until shrimp is opaque, turning occasionally. Remove basket from grill; add shrimp to butter mixture and toss to coat. Meanwhile, grill asparagus spears 5-7 minutes or until cooked but still slightly firm. Remove asparagus from grill.

4. To serve, cut asparagus on a bias into 1-in. (2.5-cm) pieces; toss with rice. Serve shrimp over pilaf.

**Yield:** 4 servings

U.S. Nutrients per serving: Calories 330, Total Fat 11 g, Saturated Fat 5 g, Cholesterol 235 mg, Carbohydrate 23 g, Protein 33 g, Sodium 1070 mg, Fiber 2 g
U.S. Diabetic exchanges per serving: 1½ starch, 4 low-fat meat (1½ carb)

## chef's corner

For an easy way to cut asparagus spears on a bias, line up the spears on the cutting board, then angle the spears on a bias. Cut the spears on a bias into 1-in. (2.5-cm) pieces using the **Utility Knife**.

Grilling the asparagus adds depth of flavor to the pilaf.

If desired, lemon pepper can be substituted for the citrus rub.

# Peanut-Crusted Pork Satay

Succulent pork tenderloin readily absorbs the savory Thai-inspired marinade and grills quickly on skewers.

### Marinade and Sauce

- ¼ cup (50 mL) soy sauce
- 2 tbsp (30 mL) fresh lemon juice
- 2 tbsp (30 mL) vegetable oil
- 2 tbsp (30 mL) packed brown sugar
- 3 garlic cloves, pressed
- ¼ tsp (1 mL) cayenne pepper
- ¼ cup (50 mL) chopped fresh cilantro
- 2 tbsp (30 mL) creamy peanut butter
- 1 tbsp (15 mL) water

### Pork

- 1 pork tenderloin (1¼ lb/625 g)
- 12 7-in. (18-cm) bamboo skewers, soaked (see Chef's Corner)
- ¼ cup (50 mL) dry roasted peanuts, finely chopped

  Bibb lettuce leaves, julienne-cut carrot and sliced radishes for *Lettuce Wraps* (optional, see Chef's Corner)

**Prep time:** 20 minutes    **Total time:** 30 minutes

1. Prepare grill for direct cooking over medium-high heat. For marinade, whisk soy sauce, lemon juice, oil, brown sugar, garlic pressed with **Garlic Press**, cayenne pepper and cilantro in **Small Batter Bowl**. Pour ¼ cup (50 mL) of the marinade into **Easy Read Measuring Cup**. Add peanut butter and water; whisk well and set aside for serving as sauce. Add remaining marinade to **Classic Batter Bowl**.

2. For pork, trim silver skin from pork. Slice pork lengthwise into two strips. Thinly slice strips crosswise; place into Classic Batter Bowl. Turn pork to coat; cover and refrigerate until ready to grill.

3. Remove pork from marinade; discard marinade. Evenly thread pork onto skewers. Grill skewers 5-6 minutes or until grill marks appear, outside of pork is deep brown and pork is barely pink in center, turning once with **BBQ Tongs**. Remove from grill. Press one side of skewers into peanuts and serve with peanut sauce as lettuce wraps, if desired.

**Yield:** 4 servings

U.S. Nutrients per serving: (3 skewers and 1½ tbsp/22 mL sauce): Calories 370, Total Fat 20 g, Saturated Fat 3.5 g, Cholesterol 90 mg, Carbohydrate 12 g, Protein 36 g, Sodium 1030 mg, Fiber 1 g
U.S. Diabetic exchanges per serving (3 skewers and 1½ tbsp/22 mL sauce): 1 fruit, 5 low-fat meat, 1 fat (1 carb)

## chef's corner

Use the **Coating Trays** to coat one side of the skewers with peanuts.

Soak skewers in water for 2 hours or overnight to prevent burning.

For *Lettuce Wraps*, prepare pork as directed. Remove lettuce leaves from 2 heads bibb lettuce. Cut 1 peeled medium carrot into julienne strips with **Julienne Peeler** and thinly slice ¼ lb (125 g) radishes with **Ultimate Mandoline**. Serve pork, carrot and radishes on lettuce leaves.

If desired, boneless, skinless chicken breasts can be substituted for the pork tenderloin. Cut into strips and thread onto skewers. Grill until chicken is no longer pink in center.

# Moroccan Grilled Meatballs with Couscous

With the help of our BBQ Grill Basket, these meatballs are smoky and full of flavor.

### Meatballs

- 3 green onions with tops (about ¾ cup/175 mL sliced)
- ¼ cup (50 mL) dry bread crumbs
- 1 egg
- 2 tbsp (30 mL) water
- 2 tbsp (30 mL) **Moroccan Rub**
- ½ tsp (2 mL) salt
- 1 lb (500 g) 93% lean ground turkey
- ⅓ cup (75 mL) apricot preserves

### Couscous

- 1½ cups (375 mL) water
- 2 tbsp (30 mL) olive oil
- 2 tbsp (30 mL) apricot preserves
- 1 tbsp (15 mL) Moroccan Rub
- 1 tsp (5 mL) salt
- 1 cup (250 mL) uncooked plain couscous
- ½ cup (125 mL) dried apricots, diced
- ¼ cup (50 mL) sweetened dried cranberries
- 1 green onion with top (about ¼ cup/50 mL sliced)

**Prep time:** 20 minutes    **Total time:** 35 minutes

1. Prepare grill for direct cooking over medium-high heat. For meatballs, in **Stainless (2-qt./2-L) Mixing Bowl**, combine green onions, bread crumbs, egg, water, rub and salt; mix until well blended. Add turkey; mix gently but thoroughly. Form meat mixture into 12 balls using level **Large Scoop**.

2. For couscous, combine water, oil, preserves, rub and salt in **Rice Cooker Plus**. Microwave on HIGH 5-6 minutes or until boiling; add couscous, dried fruit and green onion. Cover rice cooker; set aside.

3. Brush **BBQ Grill Basket** with vegetable oil; preheat on grill 3 minutes. Add meatballs and grill, covered, 5-7 minutes or until meatballs are firm. Shake basket using **BBQ Tongs** to loosen meatballs; turn meatballs over. Grill an additional 7-10 minutes, shaking basket occasionally, until meatballs are browned all the way around and **Pocket Thermometer** registers 165°F (74°C). Remove basket from grill.

4. To serve, place preserves into **Prep Bowl**; microwave on HIGH 30-45 seconds or until hot. Fluff couscous with a fork. Divide couscous among serving bowls; top with meatballs. Spoon preserves over meatballs.

**Yield:** 4 servings

LIGHT • U.S. Nutrients per serving (3 meatballs and ¾ cup/175 mL couscous): Calories 590 (24% from fat), Total Fat 16 g, Saturated Fat 3.5 g, Cholesterol 120 mg, Carbohydrate 83 g, Protein 31 g, Sodium 1450 mg, Fiber 5 g
U.S. Diabetic exchanges per serving (3 meatballs and ¾ cup/175 mL couscous): 4 starch, 1 fruit, 4 low-fat meat (5 carb)

## chef's corner

Grilling meatballs in the grill basket is an unconventional cooking method that adds flavor. Don't turn the meatballs too soon; let them firm up before shaking the basket so they keep their shape.

There is no direct substitution for our Moroccan Rub, but substituting curry powder will give this dish a nice Indian flavor.

# Dilled Tilapia with Julienne Vegetables

A medley of fresh vegetables in place of pasta is a nice accompaniment for seasoned tilapia fillets.

## Vinaigrette

- ¼ cup (50 mL) dry white wine such as Sauvignon Blanc
- 2 tbsp (30 mL) fresh lemon juice
- 2 tbsp (30 mL) olive oil
- 2 garlic cloves, pressed
- ½ tsp (2 mL) salt
- ½ tsp (2 mL) **All-Purpose Dill Mix**

## Vegetables and Tilapia

- 2 large zucchini
- 1 medium carrot, peeled
- 1 small red bell pepper
- 4 tilapia fillets (4-6 oz/125-175 g each)
- ½ tsp (2 mL) salt
- ½ tsp (2 mL) All-Purpose Dill Mix
- ¼ tsp (1 mL) coarsely ground black pepper
- Olive oil

**Prep time:** 15 minutes    **Total time:** 25 minutes

1. Prepare grill for direct cooking over medium-high heat. For vinaigrette, whisk together ingredients in **Small Batter Bowl**; set aside.

2. For vegetables, cut zucchini and carrot into julienne strips with **Julienne Peeler**. Slice bell pepper into thin strips with **Santoku Knife**. Place vegetables into **Large Micro-Cooker®** and set aside.

3. Season tilapia with salt, dill mix and black pepper; lightly spray with olive oil. Grill tilapia, covered, 3 minutes or until grill marks appear. Turn tilapia over using **BBQ Jumbo Turner**; grill 3-4 minutes or until tilapia flakes easily with a fork.

4. Meanwhile, microwave vegetables, covered, on HIGH 3-4 minutes or until crisp-tender. Microwave vinaigrette on HIGH 1½-2 minutes or until mixture comes to a boil. Divide vegetables evenly among serving plates; top with tilapia and drizzle with warm vinaigrette.

**Yield:** 4 servings

U.S. Nutrients per serving: Calories 210, Total Fat 8 g, Saturated Fat 1.5 g, Cholesterol 55 mg, Carbohydrate 9 g, Protein 24 g, Sodium 650 mg, Fiber 3 g
U.S. Diabetic exchanges per serving: 2 vegetable, 3 low-fat meat (0 carb)

## chef's corner

The Julienne Peeler makes quick work of cutting vegetables into thin strips. Use julienne-cut vegetables as a fresh, colorful side dish.

Though originally hailing from Africa, tilapia are currently farm-raised worldwide for their slightly sweet flavor and fine texture. Tilapia is firm enough to hold up to grilling. Salmon can be substituted for the tilapia, if desired.

For vinaigrette, ¼ tsp (1 mL) dried dill weed can be substituted for the All-Purpose Dill Mix. For tilapia, ¼ tsp (1 mL) dried dill weed can be substituted for the dill mix.

31

# Rosemary Pork Tenderloin

For maximum efficiency, prepare the pork while the potatoes cook in the microwave. Start grilling the pork, then skewer the potatoes and add them to the grill.

## Potatoes

10 petite red potatoes, cut in half

10 slices bacon, cut in half

## Pork

1 pkg (.75 oz/20 g) fresh rosemary, divided (7-8 sprigs)

1 tbsp (15 mL) olive oil

1 garlic clove, pressed

1 pork tenderloin (1¼ lb/625 g)

Salt and coarsely ground black pepper

**Prep time:** 20 minutes    **Total time:** 40 minutes

1. Prepare grill for direct cooking over medium-high heat. For potatoes, place potatoes and enough water to cover in **Large Micro-Cooker®**. Microwave, covered, on HIGH 7-9 minutes or until potatoes are tender; drain. Wrap one potato half with half of a slice of bacon. Immediately thread five potato halves, cut sides down, onto each of four **BBQ Skewers**, threading through bacon to hold it in place.

2. For pork, set aside six sprigs of rosemary. Finely chop remaining rosemary using **Santoku Knife** to measure ½ tsp (2 mL). In **Prep Bowl**, combine chopped rosemary, oil and garlic. Trim silver skin from pork. Brush with oil mixture using **Chef's Silicone Basting Brush**; season with salt and black pepper. Tie pork with three pieces of butcher's twine. Slide rosemary sprigs under twine (see Chef's Corner).

3. Grill pork, covered, 10 minutes or until grill marks appear. Turn using **BBQ Tongs**. Add skewers; grill 9-12 minutes or until bacon is crisp and **Pocket Thermometer** inserted into pork registers 155°F (68°C) for medium doneness. (Turn skewers as needed to cook evenly and avoid flare-ups.) Transfer skewers and pork from grill to **Cutting Board**, tent with foil and let stand 10 minutes (temperature will rise about 5°F). Slice pork; serve with potatoes.

**Yield:** 4 servings

U.S. Nutrients per serving: Calories 380, Total Fat 16 g, Saturated Fat 5 g, Cholesterol 105 mg, Carbohydrate 22 g, Protein 38 g, Sodium 470 mg, Fiber 3 g
U.S. Diabetic exchanges per serving: 1½ starch, 4½ low-fat meat, ½ fat (1½ carb)

## chef's corner

Tuck the smaller end of the tenderloin under to create a uniform thickness, then tie it with butcher's twine. Slide rosemary sprigs under the twine.

To avoid flare-ups when grilling the bacon-wrapped potatoes, make sure to place them around the outside edge of the grill where the heat is less intense. If flare-ups do occur, carefully move the potatoes to another part of the grill grid.

# Asian Grilled Chicken Rolls

Carrot and zucchini ribbons are too pretty to hide, so they are rolled on the outside of these grilled spirals.

### Glaze

- 3 tbsp (45 mL) honey
- 2 tbsp (30 mL) soy sauce
- 1 tbsp (15 mL) rice vinegar
- 1 garlic clove, pressed
- 1 tbsp (15 mL) **Asian Seasoning Mix**

### Chicken Rolls

- 12 chicken tenders (about 1½ lb/750 g)
- 1 tbsp (15 mL) Asian Seasoning Mix
- 2 tbsp (30 mL) soy sauce
- 2 large carrots, peeled
- 2 medium zucchini

### Rice

- 1½ cups (375 mL) uncooked jasmine rice
- 3 cups (750 mL) water
- 2 green onions with tops (about ½ cup/125 mL sliced)

**Prep time:** 25 minutes    **Total time:** 30 minutes

1. Prepare grill for direct cooking over medium-high heat. For glaze, whisk together ingredients in **Small Batter Bowl**. Microwave, uncovered, on HIGH 1-2 minutes until mixture comes to a boil and is slightly thickened. Set glaze aside for serving.

2. For rolls, flatten chicken to an even ¼-in. (6-mm) thickness using flat side of **Meat Tenderizer**. Combine chicken tenders, seasoning mix and soy sauce in **Stainless (4-qt./4-L) Mixing Bowl**; stir to coat.

3. Cut carrots and zucchini into long ribbons using **Vegetable Peeler**. For each roll, stack a wide carrot ribbon, zucchini ribbon and chicken tender. Roll up and secure with wooden pick. Repeat with additional carrot and zucchini ribbons and remaining chicken tenders. Spray rolls with vegetable oil using **Kitchen Spritzer**. Thinly slice remaining carrot and zucchini ribbons crosswise to measure about 1 cup (250 mL).

4. For rice, combine rice, water, remaining vegetables and green onions in **Rice Cooker Plus**. Microwave according to package directions. Meanwhile, grill rolls, chicken end down, 3 minutes or until grill marks appear. Turn over using **BBQ Tongs** and grill 2-4 minutes or until **Pocket Thermometer** registers 170°F (77°C) when inserted into center of each roll through side.

5. To serve, divide rice among serving plates; top with rolls and drizzle with glaze.

**Yield:** 4 servings

**LIGHT** • U.S. Nutrients per serving: Calories 370 (2% from fat), Total Fat 1 g, Saturated Fat 0 g, Cholesterol 100 mg, Carbohydrate 48 g, Protein 45 g, Sodium 1060 mg, Fiber 3 g
U.S. Diabetic exchanges per serving: 2 starch, 1 fruit, 1 vegetable, 5 low-fat meat (3 carb)

## chef's corner

Stack a wide carrot ribbon, then a zucchini ribbon and a chicken tender, then roll it up wide end first and secure with a wooden pick. When grilling, stand rolls up and place them onto the grid of the grill, chicken end down. This prevents the vegetables from sticking to the grill grid and tearing.

If desired, 1 tsp (5 mL) grated fresh gingerroot and an additional garlic clove, pressed, can be substituted for the Asian Seasoning Mix.

# Greek Islands Steak Salad

Chopped kalamata olives and pepperoncini peppers add depth and authenticity to this hearty salad's dressing.

### Steak

- 1½ lb (750 g) beef flank steak
- 1 tbsp (15 mL) olive oil
- 1 tbsp (15 mL) **Greek Rub**

### Dressing

- 3 tbsp (45 mL) olive oil
- 2 tbsp (30 mL) red wine vinegar
- 1 tsp (5 mL) Greek Rub
- 1 large garlic clove, pressed
- 2 tbsp (30 mL) pitted, chopped kalamata olives
- 2 tbsp (30 mL) chopped pepperoncini peppers

### Salad

- 6 cups (1.5 L) fresh baby spinach leaves
- ½ cup (125 mL) diced seedless cucumber
- ¼ cup (50 mL) crumbled feta cheese
- Additional sliced pepperoncini peppers and kalamata olives (optional)

**Prep time:** 20 minutes    **Total time:** 30 minutes

1. Prepare grill for direct cooking over medium-high heat. For steak, brush steak with oil; sprinkle with rub and press into meat. Let stand until ready to grill.

2. For dressing, whisk together ingredients in **Small Batter Bowl**; set aside.

3. Grill steak, covered, 4 minutes or until grill marks appear. Turn with **BBQ Tongs** and grill 4-6 minutes or until **Pocket Thermometer** registers 140°F (60°C) for medium-rare or 150°F (65°C) for medium doneness. Transfer steak from grill to cutting board; tent with foil and let stand 10 minutes (temperature will rise about 5°F). Slice steak across the grain into ¼-in. (6-mm) slices.

4. For salad, toss spinach and cucumber with half of the dressing in **Stainless (4-qt./4-L) Mixing Bowl**. To serve, divide salad among serving plates; arrange steak on top. Drizzle steak with remaining dressing. Top with feta cheese and additional peppers and olives, if desired.

**Yield:** 4 servings

U.S. Nutrients per serving: Calories 410, Total Fat 27 g, Saturated Fat 8 g, Cholesterol 75 mg, Carbohydrate 5 g, Protein 36 g, Sodium 590 mg, Fiber 2 g
U.S. Diabetic exchanges per serving: 1 vegetable, 5 medium-fat meat (0 carb)

## chef's corner

Flank steak is a flat, flavorful cut of beef that can be tough if overcooked. Once cooked, carve it diagonally across the grain so that the slices are tender, rather than stringy. To cut diagonally across the grain, check for the direction the meat fibers are running, then cut crosswise into thin slices, angling the knife slightly.

For the dressing, ½ tsp (2 mL) lemon zest, ⅛ tsp (0.5 mL) salt, ¼ tsp (1 mL) coarsely ground black pepper and ⅛ tsp (0.5 mL) dried oregano leaves can be substituted for the Greek Rub, if desired. Season steak with salt and coarsely ground black pepper to taste.

# Chipotle-Rubbed Beef Filets

It is possible to prepare steaks and mashed sweet potatoes in 30 minutes. Start the sweet potatoes, then get the steaks on the grill. While the steaks are resting, finish the potatoes.

**Potatoes**

- 2 medium sweet potatoes (about 12 oz/350 g each)
- ½ cup (125 mL) milk
- 2 tbsp (30 mL) butter
- ½ tsp (2 mL) salt
- 1 green onion with top (about ¼ cup/50 mL thinly sliced)
- ¼ cup (50 mL) sour cream
  Green onion curls (optional, see Chef's Corner)

**Steaks**

- 4 beef tenderloin filets (4-6 oz/125-175 g each), cut about 2 in. (5 cm) thick
- 1 tbsp (15 mL) vegetable oil
- 2 tbsp (30 mL) **Chipotle Rub**

## chef's corner

Using a kitchen towel, carefully squeeze the sweet potatoes to make sure they are very soft before mashing. The **Core & More** is a great tool to scoop out the flesh.

To make a green onion curl garnish, cut off and discard the white part of a green onion. Using the **Paring Knife**, cut the green part of the onion into thin, vertical strips. Place the strips into a **Prep Bowl** filled with ice-cold water. Let stand until the strips are curled.

For more heat, add up to 1 tbsp (15 mL) additional Chipotle Rub to the steaks.

Taco seasoning mix can be substituted for the Chipotle Rub, if desired.

**Prep time:** 20 minutes    **Total time:** 30 minutes

1. Prepare grill for direct cooking over medium-high heat. For potatoes, pierce potatoes in several places with a fork; place onto microwave-safe plate. Microwave on HIGH 14-16 minutes or until potatoes are very tender. Transfer potatoes to **Cutting Board** and cool slightly. In **Easy Read Measuring Cup**, combine milk, butter and salt. Microwave on HIGH 1-2 minutes or until hot (watch carefully to avoid boil-over). Cut potatoes in half lengthwise; scoop out flesh into **Small Batter Bowl**. Add milk mixture; mash using **Mix 'N Masher** until smooth. Cover; set aside and keep warm.

2. For steaks, brush steaks with oil. Sprinkle with rub and press into meat. Grill steaks, covered, 4 minutes or until grill marks appear. Turn with **BBQ Tongs** and grill 4-6 minutes or until **Pocket Thermometer** registers 140°F (60°C) for medium-rare or 150°F (65°C) for medium doneness. Transfer steaks from grill to serving platter; tent with foil and let stand 10 minutes (temperature will rise about 5°F).

3. Thinly slice green onion and combine with sour cream in small bowl. Serve steaks with potatoes; top with sour cream mixture. Garnish with green onion curls, if desired.

**Yield:** 4 servings

U.S. Nutrients per serving: Calories 630, Total Fat 39 g, Saturated Fat 17 g, Cholesterol 110 mg, Carbohydrate 44 g, Protein 25 g, Sodium 790 mg, Fiber 2 g
U.S. Diabetic exchanges per serving: 3 starch, 2 high-fat meat, 4 fat (3 carb)

# Grilling Tips

## Getting Started

- If using a gas grill, preheat it according to the manufacturer's directions (10-20 minutes).
- If using a charcoal grill, light the coals (about 50 briquettes) before you begin recipe preparation. You will be ready to spread out the coals when they are evenly coated with ash (20-30 minutes).
- Spread the hot coals evenly over the fire grid in a single layer, covering the entire surface evenly.
- For medium-high heat grilling, used for all recipes in this collection, wait 10 minutes after spreading out the coals before adding foods.
- Lightly coat the grill grid with vegetable oil or cooking spray before preheating the grid. Never spray vegetable oil directly over the hot grill.
- To prevent sticking and to develop better grill marks, make sure to allow the grill grid to preheat for at least 5 minutes before grilling.

## Great Grilling

- There are many variables that can affect a grill's performance. Use grilling times as guidelines. Cool or extremely hot weather, wind and higher altitudes can affect grilling times.
- Keep the grill lid closed when not turning or transferring food to maintain heat, reduce grilling time and keep flare-ups to a minimum.
- Watch foods carefully. Hot spots are common in both charcoal and gas grills. Move foods around as necessary to cook them evenly.
- These recipes call for quick-cooking foods that are cooked directly over the coals. Grilling over direct heat can cause foods to *appear* cooked before they actually are. The best way to determine doneness is to use a **Pocket Thermometer**. Insert it horizontally into the side of the food at the thickest point.
- Charcoal grills stay hot for 30-40 minutes before the coals start to burn down. Utilize the residual heat by grilling foods such as chicken breasts and vegetables for tomorrow's dinner while the grill is still hot.